SCOTS POEMS

BY

ROBERT FERGUSSON

SCOTS POEMS

BY

ROBERT FERGUSSON

SELECTED AND EDITED
BY ALEXANDER LAW, M.A.
AND PUBLISHED FOR
THE SALTIRE SOCIETY

First Edition . . . 1947
Reprinted 1974

ISBN 0 85411 022 4

Printed in Great Britain by
T. & A. Constable Ltd., Edinburgh

INTRODUCTION

ROBERT FERGUSSON, the son of Aberdeenshire parents, was born in Edinburgh on September 5, 1750. His father, William Fergusson, was a clerk and held various posts in Edinburgh and its neighbourhood. The poet was born in Cap and Feather Close, off Halkerston's Wynd, an old part of the High Street which was removed when the North Bridge was built. He was brought up in the heart of the old town whose laureate he became.

Robert Fergusson became a pupil at the High School of Edinburgh in 1758, and three years later, being presented with the Fergusson of Strathmartine bursary, proceeded to the High School of Dundee and later to St Andrews University. His stay at the University ended with his father's death in 1768, and after a visit of some months to his mother's relations in Aberdeenshire he returned to his native city. He found employment first in the Sheriff Clerk's Office and later in the Commissary Clerk's Office, monotonous work probably, but giving him a contact with the business and legal life of Edinburgh which he describes so racily in his poems.

Edinburgh in these days was a city of social clubs, and the records that remain of Fergusson's life show that he entered with spirit into the half-bohemian life associated with them. He was a member of the Cape Club, where he mixed with a varied company including the painters Runciman and Raeburn, the antiquaries David Herd and James Cummyng, and local poetasters well known in Edinburgh in their time but now forgotten. Glimpses of their jovial evenings,

> " While round they gar the bicker roll
> To weet their mouth "

are frequent in his poems, and we may feel sure that his wit made him a popular figure in this tavern life.

He first appeared as a poet with verses in English, fashionable, correct, and rather spiritless, in Walter Ruddiman's *Weekly Magazine and Edinburgh Amusement* in February 1771, but in "The Daft-Days" which the same magazine published on January 2, 1772, Fergusson wrote in Scots, vigorously and amusingly, on the Edinburgh life he knew, and his readers must have realised that a successor to Ramsay had arrived. In the poems that followed during the next two years he revived the Scots tradition of verse, and set a standard for the great poet who in his turn succeeded him.

Unlike Ramsay and Burns, Fergusson is not in the tradition of the ballad-writers ; he wrote no narrative poems and no songs. Some of his nature pieces, notably those in this volume, show pleasure in the country life and an accurate eye, but he is most at home in the town. He enjoys describing the dirt, the excitement, the crowds, the jostling, coarse life of Edinburgh, and its food and drink. The scene of "Leith Races," for example, is vividly alive with its tinkers and tradesfolk, the Lyon King of Arms, the Buchan fisher-folk speaking in their own dialect, and the town guard, "that black banditti," with their Highland accents. He is at his best in humorous descriptions of this kind, and in vituperative use of the vernacular often rivals Burns. Readers of these poems will frequently come across words and phrases which recall the works of Burns, and will find a comparison of "The Farmer's Ingle" with "The Cottar's Saturday Night," and "Leith Races" with "The Holy Fair" indicative of the debt which Burns generously acknowledged to his young predecessor.

Robert Fergusson was not of a strong constitution, and in 1774 suffered a breakdown which appears to have taken the form of religious melancholy. He recovered, but had a relapse and died miserably in the Darien House, the Edinburgh bedlam, on October 16, 1774. He is buried in the Canongate burying-ground and on his grave is a stone placed there by Burns.

The text of Fergusson suffered at the hands of editors during the nineteenth century, and this edition is based on the only reliable version, that of my old teacher, Professor Bruce Dickins, published by the Porpoise Press in 1925. I am proud to acknowledge my debt to him. For the glossary I have to thank my friend Dr John W. Oliver, for whose help in this, as in other matters, I am deeply grateful.

A. L.

CONTENTS

THE DAFT-DAYS.

Now mirk December's dowie face
Glours our the rigs wi' sour grimace,
While, thro' his *minimum* of space,
   The bleer-ey'd sun,
Wi' blinkin light and stealing pace,
   His race doth run.

From naked groves nae birdie sings,
To shepherd's pipe nae hillock rings,
The breeze nae od'rous flavour brings
   From *Borean* cave,
And dwyning nature droops her wings,
   Wi' visage grave.

Mankind but scanty pleasure glean
Frae snawy hill or barren plain,
Whan Winter, 'midst his nipping train,
   Wi' frozen spear,
Sends drift owr a' his bleak domain,
   And guides the weir.

Auld Reikie ! thou'rt the canty hole,
A bield for mony caldrife soul,
Wha snugly at thine ingle loll,
   Baith warm and couth :
While round they gar the bicker roll
   To weet their mouth.

When merry *Yule-day* comes, I trow
You'll scantlins find a hungry mou' ;
Sma' are our cares, our stamacks fou
   O' gusty gear,
And kickshaws, strangers to our view,
   Sin Fairn-year.

Ye browster wives, now busk ye bra,
And fling your sorrows far awa' ;
Then come and gies the tither blaw
   Of reaming ale,
Mair precious than the well of *Spa*,
    Our hearts to heal.

Then, tho' at odds wi' a' the warl',
Amang oursells we'll never quarrel ;
Tho' Discord gie a canker'd snarl
   To spoil our glee,
As lang's there's pith into the barrel
    We'll drink and 'gree.

Fidlers, your pins in temper fix,
And roset weel your fiddle-sticks,
But banish vile Italian tricks
   From out your quorum :
Nor *fortes* wi' *pianos* mix,
    Gie's *Tulloch Gorum*.

For nought can cheer the heart sae weil
As can a canty Highland reel,
It even vivifies the heel
   To skip and dance :
Lifeless is he wha canna feel
    Its influence.

Let mirth abound, let social cheer
Invest the dawning of the year ;
Let blithesome innocence appear
   To crown our joy,
Nor envy wi' sarcastic sneer
    Our bliss destroy.

And thou, great god of *Aqua Vitæ* !
Wha sways the empire of this city,
When fou we're sometimes capernoity,
   Be thou prepar'd
To hedge us frae that black banditti,
    The City-Guard.

CALLER OYSTERS.

Happy the man who, free from care and strife,
In silken or in leathern purse retains
A splendid shilling. He nor hears with pain
New oysters cry'd, nor sighs for chearful ale.
                                    PHILLIPS.

OF a' the waters that can hobble
A fishin yole or salmon coble,
And can reward the fishers trouble,
                    Or south or north
There's nane sae spacious and sae noble
                    As Firth o' *Forth.*

In her the skate and codlin sail,
The eil fou souple wags her tail,
Wi' herrin, fleuk, and mackarel,
                    And whitens dainty :
Their spindle-shanks the labsters trail,
                    Wi' partans plenty.

AULD REIKIE's sons blyth faces wear ;
September's merry month is near,
That brings in Neptune's caller cheer,
                    New oysters fresh ;
The halesomest and nicest gear
                    Of fish or flesh.

O ! then we needna gie a plack
For dand'ring mountebank or quack,
Wha o' their drogs sae bauldly crack,
                    And spred sic notions,
As gar their feckless patient tak
                    Their stinkin potions.

Come prie, frail man ! for gin thou *art sick,*
The oyster is a rare cathartic,
As ever doctor patient gart lick
                    To cure his ails ;
Whether you hae the head or heart-ake,
                    It ay prevails.

Ye tiplers, open a' your poses,
Ye wha are faush'd wi' plouky noses,
Fling owr your craig sufficient doses,
              You'll thole a hunder,
To fleg awa' your simmer roses,
              And naething under.

Whan big as burns the gutters rin,
Gin ye hae catcht a droukit skin,
To *Luckie Middlemist's* loup in,
              And sit fu snug
Oe'r oysters and a dram o' gin,
              Or haddock lug.

When auld Saunt Giles, at aught o' clock,
Gars merchant lowns their chopies lock,
There we adjourn wi' hearty fock
              To birle our bodles,
And get wharewi' to crack our joke,
              And clear our noddles.

Whan *Phœbus* did his windocks steek,
How aften at that *ingle* cheek
Did I my frosty fingers beek,
              And taste gude fare ?
I trow there was nae hame to seek
              Whan steghin there.

While glakit fools, o'er rife o' cash,
Pamper their weyms wi' fousom trash,
I think a chiel may gayly pass ;
              He's no ill boden
That gusts his gabb wi' oyster sauce,
              And *hen* weel soden.

At *Musselbrough*, and eke *Newhaven*,
The fisher-wives will get *top livin*,
When *lads* gang out on Sunday's even
              To treat their *joes*,
And tak of fat pandours a prieven,
              Or *mussel brose :*

Than sometimes 'ere they flit their *doup*,
They'll ablins a' their *siller* coup
For liquor clear frae cutty stoup,
        To weet their wizen,
And swallow o'er a dainty soup,
        For fear they gizzen.

A' ye wha canna stand sae sicker,
Whan twice you've toom'd the big-ars'd
Mix *caller oysters* wi' your liquor,   [bicker,
        And I'm your debtor,
If greedy *priest* or drowthy *vicar*
        Will thole it better.

BRAID CLAITH.

YE wha are fain to hae your name
Wrote in the bonny book of fame,
Let merit nae pretension claim
        To laurel'd wreath,
But hap ye weel, baith back and wame,
        In gude Braid Claith.

He that some ells o' this may fa,
An' slae-black hat on pow like snaw,
Bids bauld to bear the gree awa',
        Wi' a' this graith,
Whan bienly clad wi' shell fu' braw
        O' gude Braid Claith.

Waesuck for him wha has na fek o't !
For he's a gowk they're sure to geck at,
A chiel that ne'er will be respekit
        While he draws breath,
Till his four quarters are bedeckit
        Wi' gude Braid Claith.

On Sabbath-days the barber spark,
Whan he has done wi' scrapin wark,
Wi' siller broachie in his sark,
    Gangs trigly, faith !
Or to the Meadow, or the Park,
    In gude Braid Claith.

Weel might ye trow, to see them there,
That they to shave your haffits bare,
Or curl an' sleek a pickle hair,
    Wou'd be right laith,
Whan pacing wi' a gawsy air
    In gude Braid Claith.

If ony mettl'd stirrah green
For favour frae a lady's ein,
He maunna care for being seen
    Before he sheath
His body in a scabbard clean
    O' gude Braid Claith.

For, gin he come wi' coat thread-bare,
A feg for him she winna care,
But crook her bonny mou' fu' sair,
    And scald him baith.
Wooers shou'd ay their travel spare
    Without Braid Claith.

Braid Claith lends fock an unco heese,
Makes mony kail-worms butter-flies,
Gies mony a doctor his degrees
    For little skaith :
In short, you may be what you please
    Wi' gude Braid Claith.

For thof ye had as wise a snout on
As *Shakespeare* or Sir *Isaac Newton*,
Your judgment fouk wou'd hae a doubt on,
    I'll tak my aith,
Till they cou'd see ye wi' a suit on
    O' gude Braid Claith.

LEITH RACES.

I.

In July month, 'ae bonny morn,
  Whan Nature's rokelay green
Was spread o'er ilka rigg o' corn
  To charm our roving een ;
Glouring about I saw a quean,
  The fairest 'neath the lift ;
Her EEN ware o' the siller sheen,
  Her SKIN like snawy drift,
          Sae white that day.

II.

Quod she, " I ferly unco sair,
  " That ye sud musand gae,
" Ye wha hae sung o' HALLOW-FAIR,
  " Her winter's pranks and play :
" Whan on LEITH-SANDS the racers rare,
  " Wi' Jocky louns are met,
" Their orro pennies there to ware,
  " And drown themsel's in debt
          " Fu' deep that day."

III.

An' wha are ye, my winsome dear,
  That takes the gate sae early ?
Whare do ye win, gin ane may spier,
  For I right meikle ferly,
That sic braw buskit laughing lass
  Thir bonny blinks shou'd gi'e,
An' loup like HEBE o'er the grass,
  As wanton and as free
          Frae dule this day.

IV.

" I dwall amang the caller springs
  " That weet the LAND O' CAKES,
" And aften tune my canty strings
  " At BRIDALS and LATE-WAKES :
" They ca' me MIRTH ; I ne'er was kend
  " To grumble or look sour,
" But blyth wad be a lift to lend,
  " Gif ye wad sey my pow'r
          " An' pith this day."

V.

A bargain be't, and, by my feggs,
  Gif ye will be my mate,
Wi' you I'll screw the cheery pegs,
  Ye shanna find me blate ;
We'll reel an' ramble thro' the sands,
  And jeer wi' a' we meet ;
Nor hip the daft and gleesome bands
  That fill EDINA's street
        Sae thrang this day.

VI.

Ere servant maids had wont to rise
  To seeth the breakfast kettle,
Ilk dame her brawest ribbons tries,
  To put her on her mettle,
Wi' wiles some silly chiel to trap,
  (And troth he's fain to get her,)
But she'll craw kniefly in his crap,
  Whan, wow ! he canna flit her
        Frae hame that day.

VII.

Now, mony a scaw'd and bare-ars'd lown
  Rise early to their wark,
Enough to fley a muckle town,
  Wi' dinsome squeel and bark.

" Here is the true an' faithfu' list
    " O' Noblemen and Horses ;
" Their eild, their weight, their height, their
    " That rin for PLATES or PURSES   [grist,
        " Fu' fleet this day."

VIII.

To WHISKY PLOOKS that brunt for wooks
    On town-guard soldiers faces,
Their barber bauld his whittle crooks,
    An' scrapes them for the races :
Their STUMPS erst us'd to *filipegs*,
    Are dight in spaterdashes
Whase barkent hides scarce fend their legs
    Frae weet, and weary plashes
        O' dirt that day.

IX.

" Come, hafe a care (the captain cries),
    " On guns your bagnets thraw ;
" Now mind your manual exercise,
    " An' marsh down raw by raw."
And as they march he'll glowr about,
    'Tent a' their cuts and scars :
'Mang them fell mony a gausy snout
    Has gusht in birth-day wars,
        Wi' blude that day.

X.

Her *Nanesel* maun be carefu' now,
    Nor maun she pe misleard,
Sin baxter lads hae seal'd a vow
    To skelp and clout the guard :
I'm sure AULD REIKIE kens o' nane
    That wou'd be sorry at it,
Tho' they should dearly pay the kane,
    An' get their tails weel sautit
        And sair thir days.

XI.

The tinkler billies i' the Bow
  Are now less eidant clinking,
As lang's their pith or siller dow,
  They're daffin', and they're drinking.
Bedown LEITH-WALK what burrochs reel
  Of ilka trade and station,
That gar their wives an' childer feel
  Toom weyms for their libation
          O' drink thir days.

XII.

The browster wives thegither harl
  A' trash that they can fa' on ;
They rake the grounds o' ilka barrel,
  To profit by the lawen :
For weel wat they a skin leal het
  For drinking needs nae hire ;
At drumbly gear they take nae pet ;
  Foul WATER slockens FIRE
          And drouth thir days.

XIII.

They say, ill ale has been the deid
  O' mony a beirdly lown ;
Then dinna gape like gleds wi' greed
  To sweel hail bickers down ;
Gin Lord send mony ane the morn,
  They'll ban fu' sair the time
That e'er they toutit aff the horn
  Which wambles thro' their weym
          Wi' pain that day.

XIV.

The Buchan bodies thro' the beech
  Their bunch of *Findrums* cry,
An' skirl out baul', in Norland speech,
  " Gueed speldings, fa will buy ? "

An', by my saul, they're nae wrang gear
  To gust a stirrah's mow ;
Weel staw'd wi' them, he'll never spear
  The price o' being fu'
        Wi' drink that day.

XV.

Now wyly wights at Rowly Powl,
  An' flingin' o' the Dice,
Here brake the banes o' mony a soul
  Wi' fa's upo' the ice :
At first the gate seems fair an' straught,
  So they had fairly till her ;
But wow ! in spite o' a' their maught,
  They're rookit o' their siller
        An' goud that day.

XVI.

Around whare'er ye fling your een,
  The Haiks like wind are scourin' ;
Some chaises honest folk contain,
  An' some hae mony a Whore in ;
Wi' rose and lilly, red and white,
  They gie themselves sic fit airs,
Like Dian, they will seem perfite ;
  But its nae goud that glitters
        Wi' them thir days.

XVII.

The LYON here, wi' open paw,
  May cleek in mony hunder,
Wha geck at Scotland and her law,
  His wyly talons under ;
For ken, tho' Jamie's laws are auld,
  (Thanks to the wise recorder),
His Lyon yet roars loud and bawld,
  To had the Whigs in order
        Sae prime this day.

XVIII.

To town-guard DRUM of clangor clear,
    Baith men and steeds are raingit ;
Some liveries red or yellow wear,
    And some are tartan spraingit :
And now the red, the blue e'en-now
    Bids fairest for the market ;
But, 'ere the sport be done, I trow
    Their skins are gayly yarkit
                And peel'd thir days.

XIX.

Siclike in ROBINHOOD * debates,
    Whan twa chiels hae a pingle ;
E'en-now some couli gets his aits,
    An' dirt wi' words they mingle,
Till up loups he, wi' diction fu',
    There's lang and dreech contesting ;
For now they're near the point in view ;
    Now ten miles frae the question
                In hand that night.

XX.

The races o'er, they hale the dools,
    Wi' drink o' a' kin-kind ;
Great feck gae hirpling hame like fools,
    The cripple lead the blind.
May ne'er the canker o' the drink
    E'er make our spirits thrawart,
'Case we git wharewitha' to wink
    Wi' een as BLUE'S a BLAWART
                Wi' *straiks* thir days !

Auld Reikie, July 21. [1773].

      * A debating society. See author's note on page 30.

The FARMER'S INGLE.

Et multo in primis hilarans convivia Baccho,
Ante focum, si frigus erit.　　VIRG. BUC.

I.

WHAN gloming grey out o'er the welkin keeks,
　　When *Batie* ca's his owsen to the byre,
Whan *Thrasher John*, sair dung, his barn-door steeks,
　　And lusty lasses at the dighting tire :
What bangs fu' leal the e'enings coming cauld,
　　And gars snaw-tapit winter freeze in vain ;
Gars dowie mortals look baith blyth and bauld,
　　Nor fley'd wi' a' the poortith o' the plain ;
　　Begin, my Muse, and chant in hamely strain.

II.

Frae the big stack, weel winnow't on the hill,
　　Wi' *divets* theekit frae the weet and drift,
Sods, peats, and *heath'ry trufs* the chimley fill,
　　And gar their thick'ning smeek salute the lift ;
The *gudeman*, new come hame, is blyth to find,
　　Whan he out o'er the *halland* flings his een,
That ilka turn is handled to his mind,
　　That a' his housie looks sae cosh and clean ;
　　For cleanly house looes he, tho' e'er sae mean.

III.

Weel kens the *gudewife* that the pleughs require
　　A heartsome *meltith*, and refreshing synd
O' nappy liquor, o'er a bleezing fire :
　　Sair wark and poortith douna weel be join'd.
Wi' butter'd *bannocks* now the *girdle* reeks,
　　I' the far nook the *bowie* briskly reams ;
The readied *kail* stand by the chimley cheeks,
　　And had the riggin het wi' welcome steams,
　　Whilk than the daintiest kitchen nicer seems.

IV.

Frae this lat gentler gabs a lesson lear ;
  Wad they to labouring lend an eidant hand,
They'd rax fell strang upo' the simplest fare,
  Nor find their stamacks ever at a stand.
Fu' hale and healthy wad they pass the day,
  At night in calmest slumbers dose fu' sound,
Nor doctor need their weary life to spae,
  Nor drogs their noddle and their sense confound,
    Till death slip sleely on, and gi'e the hindmost
    wound.

V.

On sicken food has mony a doughty deed
  By Caledonia's ancestors been done ;
By this did mony wight fu' weirlike bleed
  In *brulzies* frae the dawn to set o' sun :
'Twas this that brac'd their *gardies*, stiff and strang,
  That bent the deidly yew in antient days,
Laid Denmark's daring sons on yird alang,
  Gar'd Scottish *thristles* bang the Roman *bays ;*
    For near our *crest* their heads they doughtna raise.

VI.

The couthy cracks begin whan supper's o'er,
  The cheering *bicker* gars them glibly gash
O' simmer's *showery blinks* and winters sour,
  Whase floods did erst their mailins produce hash :
'Bout *kirk* and *market* eke their tales gae on,
  How *Jock* woo'd *Jenny* here to be his bride,
And there how *Marion*, for a bastard son,
  Upo' the *cutty-stool* was forc'd to ride,
    The waefu' scald o' our *Mess John* to bide.

VII.

The fient a chiep's amang the bairnies now ;
  For a' their anger's wi' their hunger gane :
Ay maun the childer, wi' a fastin mou',
  Grumble and greet, and make an unco mane,

In rangles round before the ingle's low :
    Frae *gudame's* mouth auld warld tale they hear,
O' *Warlocks* louping round the *Wirrikow*,
    O' gaists that win in glen and kirk-yard drear,
    Whilk touzles a' their tap, and gars them shak wi'
      fear.

VIII.

For weel she trows that fiends and fairies be
    Sent frae the de'il to fleetch us to our ill ;
That ky hae tint their milk wi' evil eie,
    And corn been scowder'd on the glowing kill.
O mock na this, my friends ! but rather mourn,
    Ye in life's brawest spring wi' reason clear,
Wi' eild our idle fancies a' return,
    And dim our dolefu' days wi' bairnly fear ;
    The mind's ay *cradled* whan the *grave* is near.

IX.

Yet *thrift*, industrious, bides her latest days,
    Tho' age her sair dow'd front wi' runcles wave,
Yet frae the russet lap the *spindle* plays,
    Her e'enin stent reels she as weel's the lave.
On some feast-day, the *wee-things* buskit braw
    Shall heeze her heart up wi' a silent joy,
Fu' cadgie that her head was up and saw
    Her ain spun cleething on a darling oy,
    Careless tho' death shou'd make the feast her foy.

X.

In its auld *lerroch* yet the *deas* remains,
    Whare the gudeman aft streeks him at his ease,
A warm and canny lean for weary banes
    O' lab'rers doil'd upo' the wintry leas :
Round him will *badrins* and the *colly* come,
    To wag their tail, and cast a thankfu' eie
To him who kindly flings them mony a crum
    O' kebbock whang'd, and dainty fadge to prie ;
    This a' the boon they crave, and a' the fee.

XI.

Frae him the *lads* their morning counsel tak,
    What stacks he wants to thrash, what rigs to till ;
How big a birn maun lie on *bassie's* back,
    For meal and multure to the *thirling mill*.
Niest the gudewife her hireling damsels bids
    Glowr thro' the byre, and see the hawkies bound,
Take tent case *Crummy* tak her wonted tids,
    And ca' the leglin's treasure on the ground,
    Whilk spills a *kebbuck* nice, or yellow *pound*.

XII.

Then a' the house for sleep begin to grien,
    Their joints to slack frae industry a while ;
The leaden God fa's heavy on their ein,
    And hafflins steeks them frae their daily toil :
The cruizy too can only blink and bleer,
    The restit ingle's done the maist it dow ;
Tacksman and cottar eke to bed maun steer,
    Upo' the cod to clear their drumly pow,
    Till wauken'd by the dawning's ruddy glow.

XIII.

Peace to the husbandman and a' his tribe,
    Whase care fells a' our wants frae year to year ;
Lang may his sock and couter turn the gleyb,
    And bauks o' corn bend down wi' laded ear.
May SCOTIA's simmers ay look gay and green,
    Her yellow har'sts frae scowry blasts decreed ;
May a' her tenants sit fu' snug and bien,
    Frae the hard grip of ails and poortith freed,
    And a lang lasting train o' peaceful hours succeed.

MUTUAL COMPLAINT of *Plainstanes* and *Causey*, in their Mother-tongue.

SINCE *Merlin* laid Auld Reikie's causey,
And made her o' his wark right saucy,
The spacious *street* and *plainstanes*
Were never kend to crack but anes,
Whilk happened on the hinder night,
Whan *Fraser's* ulie tint its light,
Of Highland sentries nane were waukin,
To hear thir cronies glibbly taukin ;
For them this wonder might hae rotten,
And, like *night robb'ry*, been forgotten,
Had na' a cadie, wi' his lanthorn,
Been gleg enough to hear them bant'rin,
Wha came to me neist morning early,
To gi'e me tidings o' this ferly.
    Ye taunting lowns trow this nae joke,
For anes the ass of Balaam spoke,
Better than lawyers do, forsooth,
For it spake naething but the truth :
Whether they follow its example,
You'll ken best whan you hear the sample.

PLAINSTANES.

    My friend, thir hunder years and mair,
We've been forfoughen late and air,
In sun-shine, and in weety weather,
Our thrawart lot we bure thegither.
I never growl'd, but was content
Whan ilk ane had an equal stent,
But now to flyte I'se e'en be bauld,
Whan I'm wi' sic a grievance thrall'd.
How haps it, say, that mealy bakers,
Hair-kaimers, crieshy gezy-makers,
Shou'd a' get leave to waste their powders
Upon my beaux and ladies shoulders ?
My travellers are fley'd to deid
Wi' creels wanchancy, heap'd wi' bread,

Frae whilk hing down uncanny nicksticks,
That aften gie the maidens sic licks,
As make them blyth to skreen their faces
Wi' *hats* and muckle maun *bon-graces*,
And cheat the lads that fain wad see
The glances o' a pauky eie,
Or gie their loves a wylie wink,
That erst might lend their hearts a clink.
Speak, was I made to dree the laidin
Of Gallic chairman heavy treadin,
Wha in my tender buke bore holes
Wi' waefu' tackets i' the soals
O' broags, whilk on my body tramp,
And wound like death at ilka clamp.

CAUSEY.

Weil crackit friend——It aft hads true,
Wi' naething fock make maist ado :
Weel ken ye, tho' ye doughtna tell,
I pay the sairest kain mysell ;
Owr me ilk day big waggons rumble,
And a' my fabric birze and jumble ;
Owr me the muckle horses gailop,
Enought to rug my very saul up ;
And coachmen never trow they're sinning,
While down the street his wheels are spinning.
Like thee, do I not bide the brunt
Of Highland chairman's heavy dunt ?
Yet I hae never thought o' breathing
Complaint, or making din for naething.

PLAINSTANES.

Had sae, and lat me get a word in,
Your back's best fitted for the burden ;
And I can eithly tell you why,
Ye're doughtier by far than I ;
For whin-stanes, howkit frae the craigs,
May thole the prancing feet of naigs,

Nor ever fear uncanny hotches
Frae clumsy carts or hackney-coaches,
While I, a weak and feckless creature,
Am moulded by a safter nature.
Wi' mason's chissel dighted neat,
To gar me look baith clean and feat,
I scarce can bear a sairer thump
Than comes frae sole of shoe or pump.
I grant, indeed, that, now and than,
Yield to a *paten's* pith I maun ;
But patens, tho' they're aften plenty,
Are ay laid down wi' feet fou tenty,
And stroaks frae ladies, tho' they're teazing,
I freely maun avow are pleasing.

For what use was I made, I wonder,
It was na tamely to chap under
The weight of ilka codroch chiel,
That does my skin to targits peel ;
But gin I guess aright, my trade is
To fend frae skaith the bonny ladies,
To keep the bairnies free frae harms
Whan airing in their nurses arms,
To be a safe and canny bield
For growing youth or drooping cild.

Take then frae me the heavy load
Of burden-bearers heavy shod,
Or, by my troth, the gude auld town shall
Hae this affair before their council.

CAUSEY.

I dinna care a single jot,
Tho' summon'd by a shelly-coat,
Sae leally I'll propone defences,
As get ye flung for my expences ;
Your libel I'll impugn *verbatim*,
And hae a *magnum damnum datum ;*
For tho' frae *Arthur's-seat* I sprang,
And am in constitution strang,

Wad it no fret the hardest stane
Beneath the *Luckenbooths* to grane ?
Tho' magistrates the *Cross* discard,
It makes na whan they leave the *Guard*,
A lumbersome and stinkin bigging,
That rides the sairest on my rigging.
Poor me owr meikle do ye blame,
For tradesmen tramping on your wame,
Yet a' your advocates and braw fock
Come still to me 'twixt ane and twa clock,
And never yet were kend to range
At *Charlie's Statue* or *Exchange*.
Then tak your beaux and macaronies,
Gie me trades-fock and country Johnies ;
The deil's in't gin ye dinna sign
Your sentiments conjunct wi' mine.

PLAINSTANES.

Gin we twa cou'd be as auld-farrant
As gar the council gie a warrant,
Ilk lown rebellious to tak,
Wha walks not in the proper track,
And o' three shilling Scottish suck him ;
Or in the *water-hole* sair douk him ;
This might assist the poor's collection,
And gie baith parties satisfaction.

CAUSEY.

But first, I think it will be good
To bring it to the *Robinhood* *,
Whare we shall hae the question stated,
And keen and crabbitly debated,
Whether the provost and the baillies,
For the town's good whase daily toil is,
Shou'd listen to our joint petitions,
And see obtemper'd the conditions.

* A new instituted society, held weekly in the Thistle Lodge, where the grand concerns of the nation are debated by a set of juvenile Cicero's [Author's note].

PLAINSTANES.

Content am I—But east the gate is
The sun, wha taks his leave of Thetis,
And comes to wauken honest fock,
That gang to wark at sax o'clock ;
It sets us to be dumb a while,
And let our words gie place to toil.

To my AULD BREEKS.

Now gae your wa's—Tho' anes as gude
As ever happit FLESH and BLUDE,
Yet part we maun—The case sae hard is,
Amang the Writers and the Bardies,
That lang they'll brook the AULD I trow,
Or neibours cry, " Weel brook the NEW ; "
Still making tight wi' tither steek,
The tither hole, the tither eik,
To bang the birr o' winter's anger,
And had the hurdies out o' langer.
    Sicklike some weary wight will fill
His kyte wi' DROGS frae doctor's BILL,
Thinking to tack the tither year
To life, and look baith haill an' fier,
Till at the lang-run death dirks in,
To birze his saul ayont his skin.

    You needna wag your DUDS o' clouts,
Nor fa' into your dorty pouts,
To think that erst you've hain'd my TAIL
Frae WIND and WEET, frae SNAW and HAIL,
And for reward, whan bald and hummil,
Frae garret high to dree a tumble.
For you I car'd, as lang's ye dow'd
Be lin'd wi' siller or wi' gowd :
Now to befriend, it wad be folly,
Your raggit hide an' pouches holey ;

For wha but kens a poet's placks
Get mony weary flaws an' cracks,
And canna thole to hae them tint,
As he sae seenil sees the mint ?
Yet round the warld keek and see,
That ithers fare as ill as thee ;
For weel we lo'e the chiel we think
Can get us tick, or gie us drink,
Till o' his purse we've seen the bottom,
Then we despise, and ha'e forgot him.

Yet gratefu' hearts, to make amends,
Will ay be sorry for their friends,
And I for thee—As mony a time
Wi' you I've speel'd the braes o' rime,
Whare for the time the Muse ne'er cares
For siller, or sic guilefu' wares,
Wi' whilk we drumly grow, and crabbit,
Dowr, capernoited, thrawin gabbit,
And brither, sister, friend and fae,
Without remeid of kindred, slay.

You've seen me round the bickers reel
Wi' heart as hale as temper'd steel,
And face sae apen, free and blyth,
Nor thought that sorrow there cou'd kyth ;
But the niest mament this was lost,
Like gowan in December's frost.

Cou'd *Prick-the-louse* but be sae handy
To make the breeks and claise to stand ay,
Thro' thick and thin wi' you I'd dash on,
Nor mind the folly of the fashion :
But, hegh ! the times' *vicissitudo*,
Gars ither breeks decay as you do.
Thae MACARONIES, braw and windy,
Maun fail—*Sic transit gloria mundi !*

Now speed you to some madam's chaumer,
That butt an' ben rings dule an' claumer,
Ask her, in kindness, if she seeks
In hidling ways *to wear the breeks?*
Safe you may dwall, tho' mould and motty,
Beneath the veil o' under coatie,
For this mair faults nor yours can screen
Frae lover's quickest sense, his ein.

Or if some bard, in lucky times,
Shou'd profit meikle by his rhimes,
And pace awa', wi smirky face,
In siller or in gowden lace,
Glowr in his face, like spectre gaunt,
Remind him o' his former want,
To cow his daffin and his pleasure,
And gar him live within the measure.

So PHILIP, it is said, who wou'd ring
O'er *Macedon* a just and gude king,
Fearing that power might plume his feather,
And bid him stretch beyond the tether,
Ilk morning to his lug wad ca'
A tiny servant o' his ha',
To tell him to improve his span,
For PHILIP was, like him, a MAN.

AULD REIKIE.

AULD REIKIE, wale o' ilka town
That *Scotland* kens beneath the moon ;
Whare couthy chiels at e'ening meet
Their bizzing *craigs* and *mou's* to weet ;
And blythly gar auld care gae bye
Wi' blinkit and wi' bleering eye :
O'er lang frae thee the Muse has been
Sae frisky on the *Simmer's* green,
Whan flowers and gowans wont to glent
In bonny blinks upo' the bent ;

But now the *leaves* of yellow dye,
Peel'd frae the *branches*, quickly fly ;
And now frae nouther bush nor brier
The spreckl'd *mavis* greets your ear ;
Nor bonny blackbird *skims* and *roves*
To seek his love in yonder groves.

Then *Reikie*, welcome ! Thou canst charm
Unfleggit by the year's alarm ;
Not Boreas, that sae snelly blows,
Dare here pap in his angry nose :
Thanks to our *dads*, whase biggin stands
A shelter to surrounding lands.

Now morn, with bonny purpie-smiles,
Kisses the air-cock o' St Giles ;
Rakin their ein, the servant lasses
Early begin their lies and clashes ;
Ilk tells her friend of saddest distress,
That still she brooks frae scouling mistress ;
And wi' her joe in turnpike stair
She'd rather snuff the stinking air,
As be subjected to her tongue,
When justly censur'd in the wrong.

On stair wi' *tub*, or *pat* in hand,
The barefoot *housemaids* loe to stand,
That antrin fock may ken how *snell*
Auld Reikie will at *morning smell* :
Then, with an *inundation big* as
The *burn* that 'neath the *Nor' Loch brig* is,
They kindly shower EDINA's roses,
To *quicken* and *regale* our *noses*.
Now some for this, wi' satire's leesh,
Ha'e gi'en auld Edinburgh a creesh :
But without souring nocht is sweet ;
The morning smells that hail our street,
Prepare, and gently lead the way
To simmer canty, braw and gay :

Edina's sons mair eithly share
Her spices and her dainties rare,
Then he that's never yet been call'd
Aff frae his pladie or his fauld.

Now stair-head critics, senseless fools,
Censure their *aim*, and *pride* their rules,
In Luckenbooths, wi' glouring eye,
Their neighbours sma'est faults descry :
If ony loun should dander there,
Of aukward gate, and foreign air,
They trace his steps, till they can tell
His *pedigree* as weel's himsell.

Whan Phœbus blinks wi' warmer ray,
And schools at noon-day get the play,
Then bus'ness, weighty bus'ness, comes ;
The trader glours ; he doubts, he hums :
The lawyers eke to cross repair,
Their wigs to shaw, and toss an air ;
While busy agent closely plies,
And a' his kittle cases tries.

Now night, that's cunzied chief for fun,
Is wi' her usual rites begun ;
Thro' ilka gate the torches blaze,
And globes send out their blinking rays.
The usefu' cadie plies in street,
To bide the profits o' his feet ;
For by thir lads Auld Reikie's fock
Ken but a *sample* o' the stock
O' thieves, that nightly wad oppress,
And make baith goods and gear the less.
Near him the lazy chairman stands,
And wats na how to turn his hands,
Till some daft birky, ranting fu',
Has matters somewhere else to do ;
The chairman willing gi'es his light
To deeds o' darkness and o' night :

It's never sax-pence for a lift
That gars thir lads wi' fu'ness rift ;
For they wi' better gear are paid,
And *whores* and *culls* support their trade.

Near some lamp-post, wi' dowy face,
Wi' heavy ein, and sour grimace,
Stands she that beauty lang had kend,
Whoredom her trade, and vice her end.
But see whare now she wuns her bread
By that which nature ne'er decreed ;
And sings sad music to the lugs,
'Mang bourachs o' damn'd whores and rogues.
Whane'er we reputation lose,
Fair chastity's transparent gloss !
Redemption seenil kens the name,
But a's black misery and shame.

Frae joyous tavern, reeling drunk
Wi' fiery phizz, and ein half sunk,
Behad the bruiser, fae to a'
That in the reek o' gardies fa' :
Close by his side, a feckless race
O' macaronies shew their face,
And think they're free frae skaith or harm,
While pith befriends their leader's arm :
Yet fearfu' aften o' their maught,
They quat the glory o' the faught
To this same warrior wha led
Thae heroes to bright honour's bed ;
And aft the hack o' honour shines
In bruiser's face wi' broken lines :
Of them sad tales he tells anon,
Whan ramble and whan fighting's done ;
And, like Hectorian, ne'er impairs
The brag and glory o' his sairs.

Whan feet in dirty gutters plash,
And fock to wale their fitstaps fash ;
At night the macaroni drunk,
In pools or gutters aftimes sunk :
Hegh ! what a fright he now appears,
Whan he his corpse dejected rears !
Look at that head, and think if there
The pomet slaister'd up his hair !
The cheeks observe, where now cou'd shine
The scancing glories o' carmine ?
Ah, legs ! in vain the silk-worm there
Display'd to view her eidant care ;
For stink, instead of perfumes, grow,
And clarty odours fragrant flow.

Now some to porter, some to punch,
Some to their wife, and some their wench,
Retire, while noisy ten-hours' drum
Gars a' your trades gae dandring home.
Now mony a club, jocose and free,
Gie a' to merriment and glee :
Wi' sang and glass, they fley the pow'r
O' care that wad harrass the hour :
For wine and Bacchus still bear down
Our thrawart fortune's wildest frown :
It maks you stark, and bauld, and brave,
Ev'n whan descending to the grave.

Now some, in *Pandemonium's* * shade,
Resume the gormandizing trade ;
Whare eager *looks*, and glancing *ein*,
Forespeak a *heart* and *stamack* keen.
Gang on, my lads ; it's lang sin syne
We kent auld *Epicurus*' line ;
Save you, the *board* wad cease to rise,
Bedight wi' *daintiths* to the skies ;
And salamanders cease to swill
The *comforts* o' a *burning* gill.

* Social club in Edinburgh at the time.

But chief, O *Cape !* * we crave thy aid,
To get our cares and poortith laid :
Sincerity, and genius true,
Of knights have ever been the due :
Mirth, music, porter deepest dy'd,
Are never here to worth deny'd ;
And health, o' happiness the queen,
Blinks bonny, wi' her smile serene.

Tho' joy maist part Auld Reikie owns,
Eftsoons she kens sad sorrow's frowns ;
What groupe is yon sae dismal, grim,
Wi' horrid aspect, cleeding dim ?
Says Death, they're mine, a dowy crew,
To me they'll quickly pay their last adieu.

How come mankind, whan lacking woe,
In *Saulie's* face their hearts to show,
As if they were a clock to tell
That grief in them had rung her bell ?
Then, what is man ? why a' this phraze ?
Life's spunk decay'd nae mair can blaze.
Let sober grief alone declare
Our fond anxiety and care :
Nor let the undertakers be
The only waefu' friends we see.

Come on, my Muse, and then rehearse
The gloomiest theme in a' your verse :
In morning, whan ane keeks about,
Fu' blyth and free frae ail, nae doubt
He lippens not to be misled
Amang the regions of the dead :
But straight a painted corp he sees,
Lang streekit 'neath its canopies.
Soon, soon will this his mirth controul,
And send d——n to his soul :
Or whan the dead-deal, (awful shape !)
Makes frighted mankind girn and gape,

* Social club in Edinburgh at the time.

Reflection then his reason sours,
For the niest dead-deal may be ours.
Whan Sybil led the Trojan down
To haggard *Pluto's* dreary town,
Shapes war nor thae, I freely ween
Cou'd never meet the soldier's ein.

If kail sae green, or herbs, delight,
Edina's street attracts the sight ;
Not Covent-garden, clad sae braw,
Mair fouth o' herbs can eithly shaw :
For mony a yeard is here sair sought,
That kail and cabbage may be bought ;
And healthfu' sallad to regale,
Whan pamper'd wi' a heavy meal.
Glour up the street in simmer morn,
The birks sae green, and sweet brier-thorn,
Wi' spraingit flow'rs that scent the gale,
Ca' far awa the morning smell,
Wi' which our ladies flow'r-pat's fill'd,
And every noxious vapour kill'd.
O nature ! canty, blyth and free,
Whare is there keeking-glass like thee ?
Is there on earth that can compare
Wi' Mary's shape, and Mary's air,
Save the empurpl'd speck, that grows
In the saft faulds of yonder rose ?
How bonny seems the virgin breast,
Whan by the lillies here carest,
And leaves the mind in doubt to tell
Which maist in sweets and hue excel ?

Gillespie's snuff should prime the nose
Of her that to the market goes,
If they wad like to shun the smells
That buoy up frae market cells ;
Whare wames o' painches' sav'ry scent
To nostrils gie great discontent.

Now wha in *Albion* could expect
O' cleanliness sic great neglect ?
Nae Hottentot that daily lairs
'Mang tripe, or ither clarty wares,
Hath ever yet conceiv'd, or seen
Beyond the line, sic scenes unclean.

On Sunday here, an alter'd scene
O' men and manners meets our ein :
Ane wad maist trow some people chose
To change their faces wi' their clo'es,
And fain wad gar ilk neighbour think
They thirst for goodness, as for drink :
But there's an unco dearth o' grace,
That has nae mansion but the face,
And never can obtain a part
In benmost corner of the heart.
Why should religion make us sad,
If good frae Virtue's to be had ?
Na, rather gleefu' turn your face ;
Forsake hypocrisy, grimace ;
And never have it understood
You fleg mankind frae being good.

In afternoon, a' brawlie buskit,
The joes and lasses loe to frisk it :
Some tak a great delight to place
The modest *bon-grace* o'er the face ;
Tho' you may see, if so inclin'd,
The turning o' the leg behind.
Now Comely-garden, and the Park,
Refresh them, after forenoon's wark ;
Newhaven, Leith, or Canon-mills,
Supply them in their Sunday's gills ;
Whare writers aften spend their pence,
To stock their heads wi' drink and sense.

While dandring cits delight to stray
To Castlehill, or public way,

Whare they nae other purpose mean,
Than that fool cause o' being seen ;
Let me to *Arthur's Seat* pursue,
Whare bonny pastures meet the view ;
And mony a wild-lorn scene accrues,
Befitting *Willie Shakespeare's* muse :
If fancy there would join the thrang,
The desart rocks and hills amang,
To echoes we should lilt and play,
And gie to *Mirth* the lee-lang day.

Or shou'd some canker'd biting show'r
The day and a' her sweets deflow'r,
To Holyrood-house let me stray,
And gie to musing a' the day ;
Lamenting what auld *Scotland* knew
Bien days for ever frae her view :
O HAMILTON, for shame ! the muse
Would pay to thee her couthy vows,
Gin ye wad tent the humble strain,
And gie's our dignity again :
For O, waes me ! the Thistle springs
In *domicile* of ancient kings,
Without a patriot to regret
Our *palace* and our ancient *state*.

Blest place ! whare *debtors* daily run,
To rid themselves frae jail and dun ;
Here, tho' sequester'd frae the din
That rings *Auld Reikie's* wa's within,
Yet they may tread the sunny braes,
And brook Apollo's cheery rays ;
Glour frae *St Anthon's* grassy hight,
O'er vales in simmer claise bedight,
Nor ever hing their head, I ween,
Wi' jealous fear o' being seen.
May I, whenever *duns* come nigh,
And shake my garret wi' their cry,

Scour here wi' haste, protection get,
To screen mysell frae them and debt ;
To breathe the bliss of open sky,
And *Simon Fraser's* bolts defy.

Now gin a lown should hae his claise
In thread-bare autumn o' their days,
St *Mary*, broker's guardian saint,
Will satisfy ilk ail and want ;
For mony a hungry writer there
Dives down at night, wi' cleeding bare,
And quickly rises to the view
A gentleman, perfyte and new.
Ye rich fock, look na wi' disdain
Upo' this ancient brokage lane !
For naked poets are supply'd
With what you to their wants deny'd.

Peace to thy shade, thou wale o' men,
DRUMMOND ! * relief to poortith's pain :
To thee the greatest bliss we owe,
And tribute's tear shall grateful flow :
The sick are cur'd, the hungry fed,
And dreams of comfort 'tend their bed :
As lang as *Forth* weets *Lothian's* shore,
As lang's on *Fife* her billows roar,
Sae lang shall ilk whase country's dear,
To thy remembrance gie a tear.
By thee *Auld Reikie* thrave and grew
Delightfu' to her childer's view :
Nae mair shall *Glasgow* striplings threep
Their city's beauty and its shape,
While our new city spreads around
Her bonny wings on fairy ground.

But Provosts now that ne'er afford
The smaest dignity to *lord*,
Ne'er care tho' every scheme gae wild
That DRUMMOND's sacred hand has cull'd :

* Lord Provost at the time when the New Town was planned.

The spacious *Brig* neglected lies,
Tho' plagu'd wi' pamphlets, dunn'd wi' cries ;
They heed not tho' destruction come
To gulp us in her gaunting womb.
O shame ! that safety canna claim
Protection from a provost's name,
But hidden danger lies behind
To torture and to fleg the mind ;
I may as weel bid *Arthur's Seat*
To *Berwick-Law* make gleg retreat,
As think that either will or art
Shall get the gate to win their heart ;
For POLITICS are a' their mark,
Bribes latent, and corruption dark :
If they can eithly turn the pence,
Wi' city's good they will dispense ;
Nor care tho' a' her sons were lair'd
Ten fathom i' the auld kirk-yard.

To sing yet meikle does remain,
Undecent for a modest strain ;
And since the poet's daily bread is
The favour of the Muse or ladies,
He downa like to gie offence
To delicacy's bonny sense ;
Therefore the stews remain unsung,
And bawds in silence drop their tongue.

REIKIE, farewel ! I ne'er cou'd part
Wi' thee but wi' a dowy heart ;
Aft frae the *Fifan* coast I've seen,
Thee tow'ring on thy summit green ;
So glowr the saints when first is given
A fav'rite keek o' glore and heaven ;
On earth nae mair they bend their ein,
But quick assume angelic mein ;
So I on *Fife* wad glowr no more,
But gallop'd to EDINA's shore.

ODE *to the* BEE.

HERDS, blythsome tune your canty reeds,
And welcome to the gowany meads
The pride o' a' the insect thrang,
A stranger to the green sae lang,
Unfald ilk buss and ilka brier,
The bounties o' the gleesome year,
To him whase voice delights the spring,
Whase soughs the saftest slumbers bring.
    The trees in simmer-cleething drest,
The hillocks in their greenest vest,
The brawest flow'rs rejoic'd we see,
Disclose their sweets, and ca' on thee,
Blythly to skim on wanton wing
Thro' a' the fairy haunts of spring.

    Whan fields ha'e got their dewy gift,
And dawnin breaks upo' the lift,
Then gang ye're wa's thro' *hight* and *how*,
Seek caller *haugh* or sunny *know*,
Or ivy'd *craig*, or *burnbank brae*,
Whare industry shall bid ye gae,
For hiney or for waxen store,
To ding sad poortith frae your door.

    Cou'd feckless creature, man, be wise,
The simmer o' his life to prize,
In winter he might fend fu' bald,
His eild unkend to nippin cald,
Yet thir, alas ! are antrin fock
That lade their scape wi' winter stock.
Auld age maist feckly glowrs right dour
Upo' the ailings o' the poor,
Wha hope for nae comforting, save
That dowie dismal house, the grave.

Then feeble man, be wise, take tent
How industry can fetch content :
Behad the bees whare'er they wing,
Or thro' the bonny bow'rs of spring,
Whare vi'lets or whare roses blaw,
And siller dew-draps nightly fa',
Or whan on open bent they're seen,
On *hether-bell* or *thristle* green ;
The hiney's still as sweet that flows
Frae thristle cald or kendling rose.

Frae this the human race may learn
Reflection's hiney'd draps to earn,
Whither they tramp life's thorny way,
Or thro' the sunny vineyard stray.
Instructive bee ! attend me still,
O'er a' my labours sey your skill :
For thee shall hiney-suckles rise,
With lading to your busy thighs,
And ilka shrub surround my cell,
Whareon ye like to hum and dwell :
My trees in bourachs o'er my ground
Shall fend ye frae ilk blast o' wind ;
Nor e'er shall herd, wi' ruthless spike,
Delve out the treasures frae your bike,
But in my fence be safe, and free
To live, and work, and sing like me.
Like thee, by fancy wing'd, the Muse
Scuds ear' and heartsome o'er the dews,
Fu' vogie, and fu' blyth to crap
The winsome flow'rs frae Nature's lap,
Twining her living garlands there,
That lyart time can ne'er impair.

Broomhouse, East-Lothian,
April 26. [1773].

ODE *to the* GOWDSPINK.

FRAE fields whare SPRING her sweets has blawn
Wi' caller verdure o'er the lawn,
The GOWDSPINK comes in new attire,
The brawest 'mang the whistling choir,
That, 'ere the sun can clear his ein,
Wi' glib notes sane the simmer's green.

Sure NATURE herried mony a tree,
For spraings and bonny spats to thee :
Nae mair the *rainbow* can impart
Sic glowing ferlies o' her art,
Whase pencil wrought its freaks at will
On thee the sey-piece o' her skill.
Nae mair thro' *Straths* in simmer dight
We seek the ROSE to bless our sight ;
Or bid the bonny wa'-flowers sprout
On yonder RUIN's lofty snout.
Thy shining garments far outstrip
The cherries upo' HEBE's lip,
And fool the tints that Nature chose
To busk and paint the crimson rose.

'Mang man, wae's-heart ! we aften find
The brawest drest want peace of mind,
While he that gangs wi' ragged coat
Is weil contentit wi' his lot.
Whan WAND wi' glewy birdlime's set,
To steal far aff your dautit mate,
Blyth wad ye change your cleething gay
In lieu of lav'rock's sober grey.
In vain thro' woods you sair may ban
Th' envious treachery of man,
That, wi' your gowden glister ta'en,
Still hunts you on the simmer's plain,
And traps you 'mang the sudden fa's
O' winter's dreery dreepin' snaws.

But mergh, alas ! to disengage
Your bonny bouck frae fettering cage,
Your free-born bosom beats in vain
For darling liberty again.
In WINDOW hung, how aft we see
Thee keek around at warblers free,
That carrol saft, and sweetly sing
Wi' a' the blythness of the spring ?
Like TANTALUS they hing you here
To spy the glories o' the year ;
And tho' you're at the *burnie's* brink,
They douna suffer you to drink.
Now steekit frae the gowany field,
Frae ilka fav'rite houff and bield,

   Ah, Liberty ! thou bonny dame,
How wildly wanton is thy stream,
Round whilk the birdies a' rejoice,
An' hail you wi' a gratefu' voice.
The Gowdspink chatters joyous here,
And courts wi' gleesome sangs his peer :
The MAVIS frae the new-bloom'd thorn
Begins his *lauds* at earest morn ;
And herd lowns louping o'er the grass,
Needs far less fleetching till his lass,
Than paughty damsels bred at courts,
Wha thraw their mou's, and take the dorts :
But, reft of thee, fient flee we care
For a' that life ahint can spare.
The *Gowdspink*, that sae lang has kend
Thy happy sweets (his wonted friend),
Her sad confinement ill can brook
In some dark chamber's dowy nook :
Tho' MARY's hand his nebb supplies,
Unkend to hunger's painfu' cries,
Ev'n beauty canna cheer the heart
Frae life, frae liberty apart ;
For now we tyne its wonted lay,
Sae lightsome sweet, sae blythly gay.

Thus FORTUNE aft a curse can gie,
To wyle us far frae liberty :
Then tent her syren smiles wha list,
I'll ne'er envy your GIRNAL's *grist ;*
For whan fair freedom smiles nae mair,
Care I for life ?   Shame fa' the hair ;
A FIELD o'ergrown wi' rankest STUBBLE,
The essence of a paltry bubble.

North-Belton, Aug. 9. [1773].

HALLOW-FAIR.

AT *Hallowmas*, whan nights grow lang,
  And *starnies* shine fu' clear,
Whan fock, the nippin cald to bang,
  Their winter *hap-warms* wear,
Near Edinbrough a fair there hads,
  I wat there's nane whase name is,
For strappin dames and sturdy lads,
  And cap and stoup, mair famous
        Than it that day.

Upo' the tap o' ilka lum
  The sun began to keek,
And bad the trig made maidens come
  A sightly joe to seek
At *Hallow-fair*, whare browsters rare
  Keep gude ale on the gantries,
And dinna scrimp ye o' a skair
  O' kebbucks frae their pantries,
        Fu' saut that day.

Here country John in bonnet blue,
  An' eke his Sunday's claise on,
Rins after Meg wi' *rokelay* new,
  An' sappy kisses lays on ;

She'll tauntin say, " Ye silly coof !
  " Be o' your gab mair spairin " ;
He'll tak the hint, and criesh her loof
  Wi' what will buy her fairin,
         To chow that day.

Here chapmen billies tak their stand,
  An' shaw their *bonny wallies ;*
Wow, but they lie fu' gleg aff hand
  To trick the silly fallows :
Heh, Sirs ! what cairds and tinklers come,
  An' *ne'er-do-weel* horse-coupers,
An' spae-wives fenzying to be dumb,
  Wi' a' siclike landloupers,
         To thrive that day.

Here Sawny cries, frae Aberdeen ;
  " Come ye to me fa need :
" The brawest *shanks* that e'er were seen
  " I'll sell ye cheap an' guid.
" I wyt they are as protty hose
  " As come frae *weyr* or *leem :*
" Here tak a rug, and shaw's your pose :
  " Forseeth, my ain's but teem
         " An' light this day."

Ye wives, as ye gang thro' the fair,
  O mak your bargains hooly !
O' a' thir wylie lowns beware,
  Or fegs they will ye spulzie.
For fairn-year *Meg Thamson* got,
  Frae thir mischievous villains,
A scaw'd bit o' a penny note,
  That lost a score o' shillins
         To her that day.

The dinlin drums alarm our ears,
  The serjeant screechs fu' loud,
" A' gentlemen and volunteers
  " That wish your country gude,
" Come here to me, and I sall gie
  " Twa guineas and a crown,
" A bowl o' *punch*, that like the sea
  " Will soum a lang dragoon
                        " Wi' ease this day."

Without the cuissers prance and nicker,
  An' our the ley-rig scud ;
In tents the carles bend the bicker,
  An' rant an' roar like wud.
Then there's sic yellowchin and din,
  Wi' wives and wee-anes gablin,
That ane might true they were a-kin
  To a' the tongues at Babylon,
                        Confus'd that day.

Whan *Phœbus* ligs in *Thetis* lap,
  Auld Reikie gies them shelter,
Whare cadgily they kiss the cap,
  An' ca't round helter-skelter.
Jock Bell gaed furth to play his freaks,
  Great cause he had to rue it,
For frae a stark Lochaber aix
  He gat a *clamihewit*,
                        Fu' sair that night.

" Ohon ! " quo' he, " I'd rather be
  " By *sword* or *bagnet* stickit,
" Than hae my crown or body wi'
  " Sic deadly weapons nicket."
Wi' that he gat anither straik
  Mair weighty than before,
That gar'd his feckless body aik,
  An' spew the reikin gore,
                        Fu' red that night.

He peching on the cawsey lay,
  O' kicks and cuffs weel sair'd ;
A *Highland* aith the serjeant gae,
  " She maun pe see our guard."
Out spak the weirlike corporal,
  " Pring in ta drunken sot."
They trail'd him ben, an' by my saul,
  He paid his drunken groat
             For that neist day.

Good fock, as ye come frae the fair,
  Bide yont frae this black squad ;
There's nae sic savages elsewhere
  Allow'd to wear cockade.
Than the strong lion's hungry maw,
  Or tusk o' Russian bear,
Frae their wanruly fellin paw
  Mair cause ye hae to fear
             Your death that day.

A wee soup drink dis unco weel
  To had the heart aboon ;
It's good as lang's a canny chiel
  Can stand steeve in his shoon.
But gin a birkie's owr weel sair'd,
  It gars him aften stammer
To *pleys* that bring him to the guard,
  An' eke the *Council-chawmir*,
             Wi' shame that day.

To the TRON-KIRK BELL.

WANWORDY, crazy, dinsome thing,
As e'er was fram'd to jow or ring,
What gar'd them sic in steeple hing
        They ken themsel',
But weel wat I they coudna bring
        War sounds frae hell.

What de'il are ye ? that I shud ban,
Your neither kin to pat nor pan ;
Nor *uly pig*, nor *master-cann*
                    But weel may gie
Mair pleasure to the ear o' man
                    Than stroak o' thee.

Fleece merchants may look bald, I trow,
Sin a' Auld Reikie's childer now
Maun stap their lugs wi' teats o' woo,
                    Thy sound to bang,
And keep it frae gawn thro' and thro'
                    Wi' jarrin' twang.

Your noisy tongue, there's nae abideint,
Like scaulding wife's, there is nae guideint :
Whan I'm 'bout ony bus'ness eident,
                    It's sair to thole ;
To deave me, than, ye tak a pride in't
                    Wi' senseless knoll.

O ! war I provost o' the town,
I swear by a' the pow'rs aboon,
I'd bring ye wi' a reesle down ;
                    Nor shud you think
(Sae sair I'd crack and clour your crown)
                    Again to clink.

For whan I've toom'd the muckle cap,
An' fain wud fa' owr in a nap,
Troth I cud doze as sound's a tap,
                    Wer't na for thee,
That gies the tither weary chap
                    To waukin me.

I dreamt ae night I saw Auld Nick ;
Quo he, " this bell o' mine's a trick,
" A wylie piece o' politic,
                    " A cunnin snare
" To trap fock in a cloven stick,
                    " 'Ere they're aware.

" As lang's my dautit bell hings there,
" A' body at the kirk will skair ;
" Quo they, gif he that preaches there
      " Like it can wound,
" We douna care a single hair
      " For joyfu' sound."

If magistrates wi' me wud 'gree,
For ay *tongue-tackit* shud you be,
Nor fleg wi' *antimelody*
      Sic honest fock,
Whase lugs were never made to drec
      Thy doolfu' shock.

But far frae thee the *bailies* dwell,
Or they wud scunner at your knell,
Gie the *foul thief* his riven bell,
      And than, I trow,
The by-word hads, " the de'il himsel'
      " Has got his due."

On seeing a BUTTERFLY *in the* STREET.

DAFT gowk, in MACARONI dress,
Are ye come here to shew your face,
Bowden wi' pride o' simmer gloss,
To cast a dash at REIKIE's cross ;
And glowr at mony twa-legg'd creature,
Flees braw by art, tho' worms by nature ?
  Like country LAIRD in city cleeding,
Ye're come to town to lear' good breeding ;
To bring ilk darling toast and fashion,
In vogue amang the flee creation,
That they, like buskit BELLES and BEAUS,
May crook their mou' fu' sour at those
Whase weird is still to creep, alas !
Unnotic'd 'mang the humble grass ;
While you, wi' wings new buskit trim,
Can far frae yird and reptiles skim ;

Newfangle grown wi' new got form,
You soar aboon your mither WORM.

Kind NATURE lent but for a day
Her wings to make ye sprush and gay ;
In her habuliments a while
Ye may your former sel' beguile,
And ding awa' the vexing thought
Of hourly dwining into nought,
By beenging to your foppish brithers,
Black CORBIES dress'd in PEACOCKS' feathers ;
Like thee they dander here an' there,
Whan simmer's blinks are warm an' fair,
An' loo to snuff the healthy balm
Whan ev'nin' spreads her wing sae calm ;
But whan she girns an' glowrs sae dowr
Frae BOREAN HOUFF in angry show'r,
Like thee they scoug frae street or field,
An' hap them in a lyther bield ;
For they war' never made to dree
The adverse gloom o' FORTUNE's eie,
Nor ever pried life's pining woes,
Nor pu'd the prickles wi' the rose.

Poor Butterfly ! thy case I mourn,
To green KAIL-YEARD and fruits return :
How cou'd you troke the MAVIS' note
For " *penny pies all-piping hot ?* "
Can Lintie's music be compar'd
Wi' *gruntles* frae the CITY-GUARD ?
Or can our flow'rs at ten hours bell
The GOWAN or the SPINK excel ?

Now shou'd our sclates wi' hailstanes ring,
What cabbage fald wad screen your wing ?
Say, fluttering fairy ! wer't thy hap
To light beneath braw Nany's cap,
Wad she, proud butterfly of May !
In pity lat you skaithless stay ?

The fury's glancing frae her ein
Wad rug your wings o' siller sheen,
That, wae for thee ! far, far outvy
Her PARIS ARTIST's finest dye ;
Then a' your bonny spraings wad fall,
An' you a WORM be left to crawl.

To sic mishanter rins the laird
Wha quats his ha'-house an' kail-yard,
Grows politician, scours to court,
Whare he's the laughing-stock and sport
Of MINISTERS, wha jeer an' jibe,
And heeze his hopes wi' thought o' bribe,
Till in the end they flae him bare,
Leave him to poortith, and to care.
Their fleetching words o'er late he sees,
He trudges hame, repines and dies.

Sic be their fa' wha dirk thir ben
In blackest BUSINESS no their ain ;
And may they scad their lips fu' leal,
That dip their spoons in ither's kail.

Auld Reikie, June 21. [1773].

HAME CONTENT: A SATIRE.

To all whom it may concern.

SOME fock, like BEES, fu' glegly rin
To bykes bang'd fu' o' strife and din,
And thieve and huddle crumb by crumb,
Till they have scrapt the dautit PLUMB,
Then craw fell crously o' their wark,
Tell o'er their turners MARK by MARK,
Yet darna think to lowse the pose,
To aid their neighbours ails and woes.

Gif GOWD can fetter thus the heart,
And gar us act sae base a part,

Shall MAN, a niggard near-gawn elf !
Rin to the tether's end for pelf ;
Learn ilka cunzied scoundrel's trick,
Whan a's done sell his saul to NICK :
I trow they've coft the purchase dear,
That gang sic lengths for warldly gear.

Now whan the DOG-DAY heats begin
To birsel and to peel the skin,
May I lie streekit at my ease,
Beneath the caller shady trees,
(Far frae the din o' Borrowstown,)
Whar water plays the haughs bedown,
To jouk the simmer's rigour there,
And breath a while the caller air
'Mang herds, an' honest cottar fock,
That till the farm and feed the flock ;
Careless o' mair, wha never fash
To lade their KIST wi' useless CASH,
But thank the GODS for what they've sent
O' health eneugh, and blyth content,
An' PITH, that helps them to stravaig
Our ilka cleugh and ilka craig,
Unkend to a' the weary granes
That aft arise frae gentler banes,
On easy-chair that pamper'd lie,
Wi' banefu' viands gustit high,
And turn and fald their weary clay,
To rax and gaunt the live-lang day.

Ye sages, tell, was man e'er made
To dree this hatefu' sluggard trade ?
Steekit frae Nature's beauties a'
That daily on his presence ca' ;
At hame to girn, and whinge, and pine
For fav'rite dishes, fav'rite wine :
Come then, shake off thir sluggish ties,
And wi' the bird o' dawning rise ;

On ilka bauk the clouds hae spread
Wi' blobs o' dew a pearly bed ;
Frae falds nae mair the owsen rout,
But to the fatt'ning clever lout,
Whare they may feed at heart's content,
Unyokit frae their winter's stent.

Unyoke then, man, an' binna sweer
To ding a hole in ill-haind gear ;
O think that EILD, wi' wyly fitt,
Is wearing nearer bit by bit ;
Gin yence he claws you wi' his paw,
What's siller for ? Fiend haet awa,
But GOWDEN playfair, that may please
The second SHARGER till he dies.

   Some daft chiel reads, and takes advice ;
The chaise is yokit in a trice ;
Awa drives he like huntit de'il,
And scarce tholes TIME to cool his wheel,
Till he's Lord kens how far away,
At Italy, or Well o' Spaw,
Or to Montpelier's safter air ;
For far aff FOWLS hae FEATHERS fair.

   There rest him weel ; for eith can we
Spare mony glakit gouks like he ;
They'll tell whare TIBUR's waters rise ;
What SEA receives the drumly prize,
That never wi' their feet hae mett
The MARCHES o' their ain estate.

   The ARNO and the TIBUR lang
Hae run fell clear in Roman sang ;
But, save the reverence of schools !
They're baith but lifeless dowy pools.
Dought they compare wi' bonny Tweed,
As clear as ony lammer-bead ?
Or are their shores mair sweet and gay
Than Fortha's haughs or banks o' Tay ?

Tho' there the herds can jink the show'rs
'Mang thriving vines an' myrtle bow'rs,
And blaw the reed to kittle strains,
While echo's tongue commends their pains,
Like ours, they canna warm the heart
Wi' simple, saft, bewitching art.
On Leader haughs an' Yarrow braes,
ARCADIAN herds wad tyne their lays,
To hear the mair melodious sounds
That live on our POETIC grounds.

Come, FANCY, come, and let us tread
The simmer's flow'ry velvet bed,
And a' your SPRINGS delightfu' lowse
On TWEEDA's bank or COWDENKNOWS,
That, ta'en wi' thy inchanting sang,
Our Scottish lads may round ye thrang,
Sae pleas'd, they'll never fash again
To court you on Italian plain ;
Soon will they guess ye only wear
The simple garb o' NATURE here ;
Mair comely far an' fair to sight
Whan in her easy cleething dight,
Than in disguise ye was before
On Tibur's, or on Arno's shore.

O BANGOUR ! * now the hills and dales
Nae mair gi'e back thy tender tales !
The birks on Yarrow now deplore
Thy mournfu' muse has left the shore :
Near what bright burn or chrystal spring
Did you your winsome whistle hing ?
The muse shall there, wi' WAT'RY eie,
Gi'e the dunk swaird a tear for thee ;
And Yarrow's genius, dowy dame !
Shall there forget her blude-stain'd stream,
On thy sad grave to seek repose,
Wha mourn'd her fate, condol'd her woes.

* Mr Hamilton of Bangour [Author's note].

CALLER WATER.

WHAN father *Adie* first pat spade in
The bonny yeard of antient Eden,
His amry had nae liquor laid in
   To fire his mou',
Nor did he thole his wife's upbraidin'
   For being fou.

A caller burn o' siller sheen,
Ran cannily out o'er the green,
And whan our gutcher's drouth had been
   To bide right sair,
He loutit down and drank bedeen
   A dainty skair.

His bairns a' before the flood
Had langer tack o' flesh and blood,
And on mair pithy shanks they stood
   Than *Noah's* line,
Wha still hae been a feckless brood
   Wi' drinking wine.

The fuddlin' Bardies now-a-days
Rin *maukin*-mad in Bacchus' praise,
And limp and stoiter thro' their lays
   Anacreontic,
While each his sea of wine displays
   As big's the Pontic.

My muse will no gang far frae hame,
Or scour a' airths to hound for fame ;
In troth, the jillet ye might blame
   For thinking on't,
Whan eithly she can find the theme
   Of *aqua font.*

This is the name that doctors use
Their patients noddles to confuse ;
Wi' *simples* clad in terms abstruse,
      They labour still,
In kittle words to gar you roose
      Their want o' skill.

But we'll hae nae sick clitter-clatter,
And briefly to expound the matter,
It shall be ca'd good *Caller Water*,
      Than whilk I trow,
Few drogs in doctors shops are better
      For me or you.

Tho' joints are stiff as ony *rung*,
Your pith wi' pain be fairly dung,
Be you in *Caller Water* flung
      Out o'er the lugs,
'Twill mak you souple, swack and young,
      Withouten drugs.

Tho' cholic or the heart-scad teaze us
Or ony inward pain should seize us,
It masters a' sic fell diseases
      That would ye spulzie,
And brings them to a canny crisis
      Wi' little tulzie.

Wer't na for it the bonny lasses
Would glowr nae mair in keeking glasses,
And soon tine dint o' a' the graces
      That aft conveen
In gleefu' looks and bonny faces,
      To catch our ein.

The fairest then might die a maid,
And Cupid quit his shooting trade,
For wha thro' clarty *masquerade*
        Could than discover,
Whether the features under shade
        Were worth a lover?

As simmer rains bring simmer show'rs,
And leaves to cleed the *birken bow'rs*,
Sae beauty gets by caller show'rs,
        Sae rich a bloom
As for estate, or heavy dow'rs
        Aft stands in room.

What makes Auld Reikie's dames sae fair,
It canna be the halesome air,
But *caller burn* beyond compare,
        The best of ony,
That gars them a' sic graces skair,
        And blink sae bonny.

On *May-day* in a fairy ring,
We've seen them round St Anthon's spring,
Frae grass the caller *dew draps* wring
        To weet their ein,
And water clear as chrystal spring,
        To synd them clean.

O may they still pursue the way
To look sae feat, sae clean, sae gay!
Than shall their beauties glance like *May*,
        And, like her, be
The goddess of the vocal Spray,
        The Muse, and me.

HORACE, Ode XI. Lib. I.

Ne'er fash your *thumb* what *gods* decree
To be the *weird* o' you or me,
Nor deal in *cantrup's* kittle cunning
To speir how fast your days are running,
But patient lippen for the *best*,
Nor be in *dowy thought* opprest,
Whether we see mare winters come
Than this that spits wi' canker'd foam.

Now moisten weel your *geyzen'd wa'as*
Wi' couthy friends and *hearty blaws ;*
Ne'er lat your *hope* o'ergang your *days*,
For *eild* and *thraldom* never stays ;
The day looks *gash*, toot aff your *horn*,
Nor care yae *strae* about the *morn*.

GLOSSARY.

Poems referred to are indicated by the following :—

    A.B.—" To my Auld Breeks."
    A.R.—" Auld Reikie."
      B.—" Ode to the Bee."
    C.O.—" Caller Oysters."
     F.I.—" The Farmer's Ingle."
    H.C.—" Hame Content ; a Satire."
    Hor.—Translation from " Horace, Ode XI. Lib.I."
    L.R.—" Leith Races."
    P.C.—" Mutual Complaint of Plainstanes and Causey."

A

Ablins, Perhaps.
Afleyd, Afraid.
Air-cock, Weather-cock.
Airths, Directions (usually *airts*).
Aits, Oats.
Amry, Cupboard.
Antrin, Occasional, chance, found here and there.
Apen, Open.
Aught, Eight.
Auld-farrant, Old-fashioned, shrewd, sagacious.
Auld Nick, The Devil.

B

Bagnets, Bayonets.
Banes, Bones.
Bang, Beat, defeat.
Bassie, An old horse.
Baudrins, -ons, An affectionate term for a cat.
Bauld, Bold.
Baxter, Baker.
Bedeen, Forthwith.
Beek, Warm (*vb.*).
Beengin, Bowing.
Beild, Shelter, refuge.
Beinly, With an air of wealth, comfort and respectability.
Bend [in phrase, *Bend the bicker*], To drink deeply.
Benmost, Innermost.
Bent, Coarse grass.
Bicker, A drinking cup.

Bien, Prosperous.
Bierdly, Beirdly, Stalwart.
Biggin, Building.
Bike, Bees' nest.
Billies, Lads, fellows.
Birk, Birch tree.
Birken, Birch (*adj.*).
Birkie, A lively, smart, self-confident person.
Birn, Load.
Birr, Force, energy.
Birsle, Scorch.
Birze, Push, drive, bruise.
Bizzin, Hissing, sizzling with heat.
Blate, Bashful.
Blaw, Blow, blast, draught.
Blawort, The blue corn-flower.
Blinks, Gleams, sparkles.
Blue gown bodies, Licensed beggars.
Bodden, Provided for.
Bodle, A copper coin worth a sixth of a penny.
Bongrace, Large bonnet, shading the eyes.
Borrowstown, Burgh.
Bourachs, Burrochs, Crowds, clusters.
Bowden, Swollen.
Bowie, Milk pail.
Braw, Fine, finely.
Brogs, Brogues.
Brook [in phrase, *Weel brook the new*], Enjoy possession of.
Browster, Brewer.
Bruik, Enjoy, endure.
Brulzie, Broil, fight.
Buik, Body.

Bure, Bore.
Burnie, Brooklet.
Busk, Dress (*vb.*).
Buskit, Dressed up, decorated.
Buss, Bush.
Byke, Bees' nest.
Byword, Proverb.

C

Cadgie, Cheerful, gay, sprightly.
Cadgily, Gaily, merrily.
Cadie, A street porter.
Cairds, Gipsies.
Caldrife, Sensitive to cold.
Caller, Fresh.
Cantrip, Magic.
Canty, Lively, cheerful.
Cap, A wooden drinking vessel.
Capernoited, Peevish, irritable.
Capernoity, Quarrelsome.
Causey, Causeway.
Cawler, Clear, fresh.
Chap, To break up (intransitive).
Chapman, Pedlar.
Chauner, Chamber, room.
Cheep, Squeak.
Chiel, Chield, Fellow.
Chimley cheeks, Sides of the hearth.
Chow, Chew.
Clamihewit, Stroke, blow.
Clarty, Filthy.
Clashes, Gossip.
Cleed, Clothe.
Cleedin, Clothing.
Cleek in, Lay hold on, capture.
Cleugh, Narrow glen, ravine.
Clour, Beat, belabour.
Clouted, Patched.
Coble, Short, flat-bottomed boat.
Cod, Pillow.
Codroch, Rustic, uncouth.
Coft, Bought.
Conveen, Come together.
Coof, Simpleton.
Coothy, Friendly, familiar, sociable.
Corbies, Crows.
Cosh, Snug.
Couli, A boy, or (familiarly or contemptuously) a man.
Coup, Upset, empty out.
Couth, Comfortable.
Couthie, -y, Snug, cosy, friendly.

Crabbitly, Acrimoniously.
Crackit, Spoken.
Craig, Crag (B.).
Craig, Throat (C.O.).
Crap, Throat.
Craw, Crow.
Creels, Baskets.
Creesh, A beating, a whipping.
Creish, Grease, oil (*vb.*).
Creishy, Greasy.
Crook, Twist, bend.
Cruizy, Oil lamp for rushlight.
Cuissers, Stallions.
Culls, Fools, gulls [cf. *Johnson* *Dictionary*, " Cully : a man deceived or imposed upon ; a by sharpers, or a strumpet "].
Cunzied, Coined, made (A.R.).
Cunzied, Moneyed, wealthy (H.C.).
Cutty, Short.
Cutty-stool, Stool of repentance.

D

Daffin, Folly, frivolity, flirting.
Daintiths, Dainties.
Dautit, Darling, pet.
Dead, Death.
Dead-deal, The board used for measuring and lifting a corpse.
Deas, Long wooden settle, which could be used as a couch or bed.
Deave, Deafen, weary out.
Deil, Devil.
Dight, Decked, dressed.
Dightin, Winnowing.
Dightit, Prepared for use, dressed.
Ding, Knock, beat, drive, excel.
Dint, Affection, taste for something.
Dirk, Grope one's way.
Divots, Turfs.
Doitet, Stupid.
Dool, Sorrow.
Dorts, Sulks, a petted mood.
Dorty, Petted, peevish.
Dought, Can.
Doughtna, Cannot bring oneself to do something.
Douk, Duck.
Doup, Buttocks.
Dour, Sullen, obstinate (A.B.).
Dour, Sternly (B.).
Dow'd, Were able (A.B.).

Dow'd, Withered, dried (F.I.).
Dowie, -y, Doleful, melancholy.
Downa, Cannot.
Doylt, Tired.
Dree, Endure, suffer.
Dreech, Dry, wearisome, tedious.
Droukit, Drenched.
Drouth, Dryness, thirst.
Drowthy, Fond of drink.
Drucken-groat, A fine for drunkenness.
Drumbly, drumly, Turbid, dull, melancholy, confused, muddled.
Duddies, Clothes.
Duds, Rags.
Dule, Sorrow.
Dules, Goals, bases in games of the baseball type.
Dung, Wearied.
Dunk, Dank, damp.
Dwaam, Qualm.
Dwynin, Dwindling, drooping.

E

Ear, Early.
Ear'est, Earliest.
Earn, Gather together.
Eidant, Diligent.
Eik, Addition, patch.
Eild, Old age.
Eild, Age (L.R.).
Eith, Easily.
Eithly, Easily.
Ell, A measure of about thirty-seven inches.

F

Fa, Who [a north-eastern form].
Fadge, Wheaten loaf.
Fairn-year, Last year.
Fash, Trouble, worry, take pains.
Fauld, Fold (*n.* and *vb.*).
Feat, Neat, tidy.
Feck, fek, Majority, plenty.
Feckless, Weak, feeble, helpless, spiritless.
Feckly, Usually, for the most part.
Fee, Wages.
Feggs! Faith!
Fells, Supplies.
Fence, Protection.
Fenzying, Feigning.
Ferly, Wonder, marvel.

Fern-year, Last year.
Fient, Devil (in exclamations).
Fier, Sound, healthy.
Filipegs, Kilt.
Findrums, Smoke-dried haddocks.
Fit, Foot.
Flee, Fly.
Fleetch, Flatter, beguile.
Fleetchen', Flattery.
Fleg, Frighten.
Fleuk, Flounder.
Fley, Affright, frighten away.
Fley'd, Frightened.
Flung, Charged.
Flyte, Scold.
Fouk, Folk, people.
Fousom, Over-rich.
Flit, Remove, change position.
Forfoughen, Worn out.
Fou, Drunk.
Fouth, Abundance.
Foy, Farewell feast.

G

Ga', Gall.
Gabb, Mouth, taste, palate.
Gantrees, Gantries, stands for barrels.
Gar, Cause, force, compel.
Gardies, Arms.
Gash, Bright (Hor.).
Gash, Chat (F.I.).
Gate, Way, road.
Gaunt, Yawn.
Gausy, Large, plump, jolly, swaggering, self-confident.
Geck, Jeer, mock, flout.
Girn, Grin, make grimaces, snarl.
Girnel, Granary, meal chest.
Gizzen, Become dry and parched.
Gizzy-makers, Wig-makers.
Glakit, Senseless, silly, irresponsible.
Gleds, Kites.
Gleg, Quick, nimble, mentally alert (*adj*).
Gleg, Readily, glibly, briskly, gaily (*adv.*).
Glent, Gleam, sparkle.
Gloamin, Twilight.
Glore, Glory.
Glowr, Stare, scowl.
Gowan, Daisy.
Gowany, Daisy-sprinkled.

Gowd, Gold.
Gowden, Golden.
Gowdspink, Goldfinch.
Gowk, Fool [literally, a cuckoo].
Graith, Accoutrements, equipment, finery.
Grane, Groan.
Gree, First place, supremacy.
Green, Yearn, aspire.
Grien, Long, yearn.
Grist, Size.
Gruntles, Gruntings.
Guard, Guard-house.
Gust, Give pleasure or relish to.
Gustit, Seasoned.
Gusty gear, Tasty food.
Gutcher, Grandfather.

H

Hack o' honour, An honourable wound.
Had, Hold, keep.
Haet, Atom, particle [in phrase, *Fient haet ava*, " Devil a bit."].
Haffits, Temples, upper cheeks.
Ha' house, Mansion house.
Haiks, Hacks, horses.
Hail, Hale, healthy.
Hail, To drive a ball to a goal or mark [in phrase, *Hail the dules*, " Reach the mark."].
Hain'd, Saved.
Hair-kaimers, Hair-dressers.
Hail, Whole.
Halflins, Half.
Halland, Partition wall between outer door of cottage and the inner part of the room to which it gave entrance.
Hap, Wrap oneself up against the cold.
Hapwarmers, Overcoats, wraps.
Harl, Drag, pull.
Hash, Damage, destroy.
Haugh, Low ground beside a river.
Hawkies, Cows.
Hauses, Throats.
Heart-scad, Heart-burn.
Heese, Lift, exalt.
Herried, Plundered, raided.
Het, Hot.
Hidling, Secret.
Hip, Omit.
Hirplin, Limping.

Hobble, Toss, shake.
Hooly, Slowly, continuously.
Horse-coupers, Horse-dealers.
Hotches, Jolts.
Houff, Haunt, place of resort.
Houkit, Dug.
Hound, Hunt.
How, Hollow, glen, valley.
Hummil, Threadbare, napless [literally, hornless].
Hunder, Hundred.
Hurdies, Hips.

I

Ilka, Every.
Ill-hained, Saved to no good purpose.
Ingle, Fire, fireplace, fireside.
Ingle cheek, Fireside.

J

Jillet, Jilt, hussy.
Joe, Sweetheart.
Jouk, Dodge, escape.
Jow, Clang, toll.

K

Kail, Cabbage, broth.
Kail-worms, Caterpillars.
Kail-yard, Vegetable garden.
Kain, Kane, Rent paid in farm produce, a penalty.
Kebbuck, Cheese.
Keek, Peep.
Keekin-glasses, Mirrors.
Kendlin, Budding.
Kill, Kiln.
Kist, Chest.
Kitchen, Relish, tasty food.
Kittle, Ticklish, delicate, subtle, difficult, dangerous.
Kniefly, Vivaciously.
Knowe, Knoll, low hill.
Kye, Cows.
Kyte, Stomach.
Kyth, Become known, appear.

L

Lade, Load, fill.
Ladin, Load, weight.
Laiglen, Milk pail.
Lammer, Amber.

Land-loupers, Wastrels, vagabonds.
Langer, Perhaps a misprint for *danger* (A.B.).
Late-wakes, The watching of a dead body.
Lavrock, Lark.
Lawen, Reckoning.
Leal, Soundly, truly (*adv.*).
Leally, Loyally, confidently.
Lear, Learn.
Leared, Taught.
Leas, Meadows.
Leem, Loom [north-eastern form].
Leesh, Lash.
Legs, Perhaps a misprint for *Fegs* (*q.v.*).
Lerroch, Position, site.
Ley-rig, An unploughed ridge in a cultivated field.
Libel, Accusation.
Licks, Knocks, blows.
Lift, Sky.
Ligs, Lies.
Limmer, Hussy.
Lintie, Linnet.
Lion, Lyon King of Arms [who, at the time " Leith Races " was written had been prosecuting persons for displaying on their carriages coats-of-arms not regularly matriculated], (L.R.).
Lippen, Trust.
Lippen for, Have faith in, expect with confidence.
Lochaber axe, Halberd.
Loof, Palm of the hand.
Loon, lown, Lad, boy, fellow, rascal.
Lounder, A heavy blow, a dull thud.
Loup, Leap.
Loup in, Look in, pay a casual visit.
Louse, lowse, Unloose, open.
Lout, Bend.
Loutit, Bent.
Lugs, Ears.
Lum, Chimney.
Lyart, Grey-haired.
Lyther, More sheltered.

M

Mailin, Small farm.
Maister can, An earthen vessel for preserving urine to be used in washing clothes.

Maksna, Matters not.
Man, Must.
Marches, Borders.
Mark, Silver coin worth 13s. 4d. Scots.
Maught, Might, strength, power.
Maukin-mad, Mad as a hare.
Maun, Very, most (*adv.*) [placed after adjectives, as in P.C., *Muckle maun*].
Mavis, Song thrush.
Meikle, Big (*adj*).
Meikle, Greatly (*adv.*).
Meltith, A meal.
Mergh, Strength, energy [literally, marrow].
Mess John, Minister.
Mirk, Dark.
Mishanter, Misfortune.
Misleared, Misguided.
Mony, Many.
Motty, Spotted.
Mou, Mouth.
Mu'ter, Multure, a toll in kind paid to a miller for grinding corn.

N

Naigs, Nags.
Nappy, strong (of liquor).
Near-gaun, Stingy, mean.
Neb, Beak.
Nick, The Devil.
Neist, Next.
Nickit, Cut.
Nick-sticks, Tallies.
Nor, Than.
Nowt, Cattle.

O

Obtempered, Fulfilled.
Or, Ere, before.
Orro, Odd, surplus, occasional.
Ouks, Weeks.
Outowre, Out from, across.
Owre, Over.
Owsen, Oxen.
Oye, Grandchild.

P

Paiks, Blows given in punishment.
Painches, Paunches, tripes.
Pandours, A large type of oyster.
Partan, A crab.

Paughty, Haughty.
Pawky, Sly.
Pechin, Panting.
Pegs, The tuning pegs of a violin (L.R.).
Penny note, A forged one pound note.
Pet, Umbrage [in phrase, *Take the pet*].
Pingle, Conflict, debate.
Plack, A copper coin worth a third of a penny.
Plainstanes, Flagged pavement.
Playfair, Toy, trifle.
Pleys, Quarrels.
Plooks, Pimples.
Plouky, Pimply.
Pomet, Pomatum.
Poortith, Poverty.
Pose, Purse, secret hoard of money.
Pow, Head.
Prick-the-louse, A tailor.
Pride, Take pride in.
Prie, Taste.
Prieven, A tasting, a sample.
Propone, Put forward (by a party to a law-suit).

Q

Quean, Damsel, lass.

R

Rangles, Clusters.
Raw, Row.
Rax, Reach out, stretch oneself, grow bigger.
Ream, To foam.
Recorder, Probably the Lyon Clerk (L.R.).
Reek, To reach (*vb.*).
Reesle, Clatter.
Reistit, With the fire made up for the night.
Rift, Belch.
Rig, Ridge (esp. in a cultivated field).
Riggin, Roof, rafters, ridge of a roof.
Robinhood, Name of an Edinburgh debating and social club.
Rokelay, Roquelaure, a cloak reaching to the knee [called after the Duke of Roquelaure (1656-1738)].
Rookit, Plundered, despoiled.

Roose, Praise, flatter.
Roset, Apply rosin to.
Rout, Low, bellow.
Rowly-powl, The game of quoits or ninepins.
Rug, Pull, wrench ; bargain.
Rung, Stick.
Runkles, Wrinkles.

S

Sain, Bless.
Saired, Served.
Salamanders, Perhaps the members of the Pandemonium Club.
Sark, Shirt.
Saul, Soul.
Saulie, A funeral mute, a hired mourner.
Scad, Scald.
Scancin, Glittering.
Scantlins, Scarcely.
Scape, Hive.
Scauld, Scolding.
Scaw'd, Scabbed.
Sclates, Slates.
Scowdered, Scorched.
Scowry, Showery, squally.
Screed aff, Reel off.
Scrimp, Give grudgingly or sparingly.
Scunner at, Be disgusted by.
Seenil, Seldom.
Sensyne, Since.
Sey, Try.
Sey-piece, Masterpiece [literally, the piece of work shown by an apprentice wishing to qualify as a journeyman].
Sharger, Thin, stunted person.
Shaw, Show.
Shellycoat, A sheriff's officer.
Sicker, Sure, steady.
Siclike, Similarly.
Siller, Silver.
Simmer roses, Inflammation of the skin.
Sinsyne, Since.
Skair, Share (*vb.* and *n.*).
Skaith, Injury, trouble, pain.
Skaithless, Unhurt.
Skar, Be afraid of.
Slae, Sloe.
Slocken, Quench.

neek, Smoke.
sell, Keen, sharp, pungent.
selly, Keenly.
sout, Face.
sck, Ploughshare.
sugh, Humming.
sup, Sip, a little drop.
sae, Foretell.
sae-wives, Women fortune-tellers.
sats, Spots.
saterdashes, Gaiters, spats.
seel'd, Climbed.
seldings, Small sun-cured fishes.
sier, Ask.
sink, The pink.
sraing, A streak of colour.
sraingit, Streaked, of varied colours.
srush, Spruce.
sulzie, Spoil, injure.
sunk, Spark.
sammer, Stagger.
sark, Stout, strong.
sarnies, Stars.
saw'd, Surfeited.
seek, Stitch (*n.*).
eek, Shut (*vb.*).
eekit, Shut out, shut up, confined.
eeve, Firm, steady.
eghin, Packing with food, guzzling.
ent, Task, a fixed allotment of work.
irrah, Sirrah, fellow.
oiter, Stumble, stagger.
oup, Drinking cup.
rae, Straw.
raik, Stroke, blow.
ravaig, Wander aimlessly.
reakit, streekit, Stretched out.
reeks, Stretches.
uck, Deprive, mulct.
wack, Nimble.
weel, Swill.
nd, Wash, wash down food, drink.

T

ack, Lease.
ackets, Hob-nails.
argets, Thin slices peeled off.
eats, Small quantities.
eem, Empty.
ent, Take note of, pay heed to.
enty, Careful.
hae, These, those.

Theekit, Thatched.
There-ben, Through to the inner room [figuratively, to the confidence of the great].
Thereout, Outside, afield.
Thir, These, those.
Thirlin mill, Mill at which tenants were bound to have their corn ground.
Thole, Bear, endure, require.
Thrang, Crowded, busy.
Thraw, Twist.
Thrawart, Froward, perverse, adverse, untoward.
Thrawn-gabbit, With twisted mouth, with a snarling expression.
Threap, Insist on, urge.
Tint, Lost.
Tither, Other.
Tongue-tackit, Tongue-tied.
Toom, Empty (*adj.* and *vb.*).
Toot, Drink off.
Top, Excellent; as in *Get top livin*, Do a first-rate trade (C.O.).
Toutit, Drank off.
Troke, Exchange, barter.
Truffs, Turfs, peats.
Tulzie, Strife, toil, trouble.
Turner, An old Scots coin, worth two pennies (Scots).
Tyne, Lose, forfeit, give up.

U

Ulie, Ulzie, Oil.
Ulzie-pig, Oil jar.
Unco, Very.
Unfleggit, Undismayed.
Unkend, Unknown.
Unkend to, Unaware of.

V

Vogie, Merry, carefree.

W

Wae, Woe.
Waesuck, Alas.
Wale, The choicest, the pick (*n*).
Wale, Choose, select (*vb.*).
Wallies, Fine looking, showy things.
Wambles, Rumbles, rolls.
Wame, weym, Stomach.
Wanchancy, Unlucky, dangerous.

Wanruly, Unruly.
Wanwordy, Worthless.
Ware, Spend.
Warlock, Wizard.
Waur, Worse.
Weir, War.
Weird, Fate.
Weirlike, Warlike.
Weyr, Wire [a phonetic rendering of the north-eastern pronunciation].
Whang'd, Cut up, sliced.
Whilk, Which.
Whinge, Whine, fret.
Whittle, Razor.
Win, Dwell.

Windocks, Windows.
Winnow't, Dried by the wind.
Wirrikow, Hobgoblin.
Wov, Wool.
Woodies, Gallows.
Wud, Mad.
Wyt, To know, assure.

Y

Yarkit, Knocked about, beaten.
Yellowchin, Screeching.
Yird, Earth.
Yole, Yawl.
Yule-day, Christmas Day.